Turnings

Turnings

Poems of Transformation

William Johnson Everett

RESOURCE *Publications* • Eugene, Oregon

TURNINGS
Poems of Transformation

Resource Publications
An Imprint of Wipf and Stock Publishers
199 W. 8th Ave., Suite 3
Eugene, OR 97401
www.wipfandstock.com

ISBN 13: 978-1-62032-735-7
Manufactured in the U.S.A.

For Sylvia,
In all our turnings

To every thing
there is a season,
and a time to every purpose
under the heaven.

—ECCLESIASTES,
OR THE PREACHER 3:1 (KJV)

Contents

Acknowledgments

For her encouragement and guidance I want to thank Kathryn Stripling Byer, former Poet Laureate of North Carolina, who continues to nurture the poetic arts and artists of our region. To my friend and fellow poet, Michael Beadle, I say thanks for many hours of mutual critique and help along the way. I am indebted to J.C. Walkup, Penny More, and Buffy Queen, whose intrepid and lively publication, *Fresh*, has publicized my poetry in our region. In addition, I have been greatly helped by the poets and writers of North Carolina who gather under the umbrella of the North Carolina Writers Network and its Netwest chapter.

"Sweet Lady" appeared previously in *Spiritus: A Journal of Christian Spirituality*, 11:1 (Spring 2011), 127. *Fresh* has published "A People Passing Over," *Fresh*, (Fall, 2009), 12; "Unconjugation" (originally "Lie, lay, lain, laid, lied,") *Fresh*, (Spring, 2010), 35; and "Earth Gasping," *Fresh* (Issue V, 2012), 31. "Glossy Expectations" and earlier versions of "Mary's Cry" and "Waiting" appeared in www.YourDailyPoem.com in 2011.

The quotation in "Kin(g)" from King James I of England is from his "True Law of Free Monarchies," [1598, 1616] . The quotation in "Kin(g)" from Sigmund Freud is from his *Totem and Taboo*, trans. A. A. Brill (London, 1919; Art & Poetry Publishing, 2011), chapter 4, section 5.

Memories

Elephants
return to the bones of their kin
now bleached by the sun,
turning them over with their trunks,
sniffing the ribs,
caressing the limbs,
leaving their footprints behind
until they return again
to turn
and be turned,
Remembered.

Elephants

Beneath the rusted roofs
    where children played
Behind gray-beaten boards
    engrained with laughter,
Below the pines that
    drape the walls
    in shadow calico,
Where sun bakes down
    the flower patch,
    smiles upon the puppies
    hushed in memory
    sleeping on the porch,
Old folks whisper in the weeds
    it was not so,
    it was not so.

Rusted Roofs

Old photographs
laid out upon the table,
glossy colors running red or blue
receding like some distant stars
shifting on the spectrum of our memory,
array themselves like Hubble's mirrors,
magnifying memories a billion times
to bring them close,
the nebulae that gave us birth.

Old Photographs

Round red lips pubaceous
　　smile in the glossy picture of the party
　　　　　frozen on the yellowing page,
　　a sentimental daiquiri
　　　　　of tender expectations.
How, with whom, and where
　　will teasing eyes find their reflection?
Who will find the woman
　　in the girl in the taffeta gown?

Glossy Expectations

If,
my dear,
I could have touched your skin
at twenty-one
and rolled you in my
hey now
freshening arms,
come face upon your glistening eyes,
your tongue
sweet laughter in my opening ear,
your heart
a hungry fire,
And most,
my dear,
my seed within your garden planted
where no stranger ever came,
I would have found,
my mate alone,
the child within
we foster here.

If, My Dear

The yawning sunset quilts our bed
    as homeward I collect myself
    and pour the pockets of my day
    upon her welcoming hands.
The dirt, the coins, the rubber bands,
    the ticket stub and napkin shred
    are offered to her eyes.
With every scrap of life
    we table in communion
    and share the harvest hour.
Surely God is bountiful!
My head runneth over.
Now my cup is full.

Offering

Where are those friends
who have drifted downstream
so far from our still grinding mill?
The first grade best friend
who built with me
castles of sand,
That summer camp comrade
who told me
why parents sleep
doubled in bed,
The roommate in college
who heard of our meeting
that breathless first time,
My best friend that year
when we broke up
and made up
and tiptoed on fragments
of innocence,
The bridesmaid who fainted in heat
from those summer day kisses
that sealed our promises,
Where have they gone
on that river downstream
where the ocean receives all the water
that powers our mill?

Where Are Those Friends?

I raised 'em best I could,
Did my best to hold 'em to their promises,
Let 'em play but kept 'em at their chores.
Worried how they handled money,
Let 'em make mistakes but told 'em what they were.
Helped 'em set the table at Thanksgiving,
Laughed with them while building Santas in the snow.
Yes, we travelled,
But I told 'em not to speak with strangers,
Called 'em back from edges of the scenic canyons,
Let 'em know how many miles to go.
Showed 'em how to operate their first computer,
Wowed 'em with my knowledge,
Planted questions in their minds.

Now they are old,
They utter words I cannot grasp,
Their diapers sagging,
Mumbling in their memories,
Waiting to be raised again.

Raisin'

Memories

Lefkarìtiko (Greek): Traditional fine lace
embroidery developed in Lefkara, Cyprus.

We didn't ask
my grandmother
about the fancy cloth,
its lacework
filigreed upon the table.
We couldn't hear
the murmurs of the village women
spelling out their lives in fullered filaments
beneath the olive trees.
We didn't ask
what was this Lefkaritiko that said
I Am.
We didn't ask
how did they live among the men
who sweated in the fields and mines,
and gathered in cafes to tell survivor tales.
My mother said
her family lived at Skouriótissa,
"Our Lady of the Slag Heaps,"
where her father was the mining engineer.
We didn't ask
my grandfather
about the oil lamps he gave us
beyond his simple statement
"These were found in ancient Roman copper mines."
We couldn't hear
the Turkish, Greek, and Russian miners
wresting them from ancient Cypriot sepulchres
within the labyrinth of abandoned shafts.
We didn't learn
about the fatal accidents
that happened on his watch

while mother only nine years old
held her precious wounded dove
beside the little church
outside their home
within abandoned monastery walls.
We didn't ask
my mother
if she ever went inside the ancient church
how dark it was
without a window
only candles opening eyes to icons
on the wall of mystery
where the priest was hidden
chanting words she couldn't understand
within that holy night behind.
We didn't know
our memory is a lacework
made of fragile threads
that put a patterned beauty
on the table of our daily bread,
how you have to tie the strings together
if you want to celebrate a meal.

Lefkaritiko

He was
a tower in the whistling wind,
a flower waving in a symphony of celebration,
a stallion heavy breathing lunging for the jump,
a tree whispering with patient supplication,
a boat slopping over choppy waters, clapping under sail,
a seashell echoing the deep.
All gone.
Now nothing
but the wind,
the same familiar wind,
wild,
warm,
enveloping,
blowing over empty ocean,
empty land.
Man still here,
mind gone.

Here and Gone

A single thread
    in the cloth bag
    holding our treasures
    breaks.
Our glistening marbles,
    photographs of younger smiles,
    address books,
    journals of our inward thoughts,
    slip through
    the widening tear.
We fall
    with them,
    wondering
    if loving hands will catch us.

A Single Thread

Jesus left no books behind,
    epistolary memories
    rolled up,
    bound over,
    binding our devotion
    to a life in mausoleums.
His lips were full of atmospheres
    evaporating in the nostrils
    of our death.
No retina retained his form,
He left no graven immortality,
Only whispers of a harmony in time.

No Books

Explore the great immensity,
    the black abyss,
    the emptiness,
    the outside of our outer space.
Find out
    do hands enfold the universe?
    do they have feet to stand?
Snap wide the bounds,
    transcend the awful hope of immortality,
    show that love created space and time.

Mentalphysics

Believe me,
  I saw death
  come gaping in
  teeth empty
  said nothing
  no reason
  to swallow us up
  in oblivion.
Drink I eat food
  and mouth water
  lip wine
  in the love
  of your flesh
  in my flesh.

I Saw Death

She laid them gently in the box,
the starry diamond brooch of Africa,
bright sapphire stones for Swedish eyes,
the silver nail necklace wrought of Navajo,
blood ruby ring from India,
the deep dark emerald hope of Israel,
the man who cried,
She laid him gently down.

Pietà

Sweet lady,
    if
    in tinseled tear
    you pray the evergreen upon us,
    supplicate the lavish laughter of your heart
    to snow upon the muddy traces of our minds.

Sweet Lady

Seasons

Chartreuse fingerprints upon the willows
    manifest advancing sun.
Charred signatures of winter's fire
    dissolve before the Spring.
The waning chapter of an Easter moon
    paints halos on the budding trees
    whose chattering branches
    charm the wakening meadowlarks,
    revealing mercy's Chartres.

Spring's Cathedral

Ants diligent desiring sweetness
    seek the peony in early Spring.
Pink petal pursed plays patient
    to their delicate petition.
Flowering mystery soft unfolding
    gives glory praise
    in blossom beauty
    following the sun,
Invokes the early honey bee
    who nectar gathering
    thanks the ant
    for birthing beauty
    out of toil.

Ants Diligent

Reticulate
her infancy
surrounds the chair.
Her gloried curls lie
in fetal invocation
on the floor.
A lady paces round her
crysallating form
with scowls,
and frowns,
and cautious smiles,
While we look on
distressed
that children have to die
to grow up beautiful.

Pubertal Sacrifice

She is ready,
    purse packed,
    one hand pocketed in resolution,
    standing by her charge.
Will she fly through puffball clouds,
    piercing azure heavens like a needle?
Or will she cruise majestically across the land,
    blowing tumbleweeds and sagebrush in her wake?
Perhaps the sea shall feel the power of her legs,
    the undulations of her mermaid form.
For she is ready,
    glowing hair pinned sleekly back,
    the keys clutched in her hand.
She is the girl with the '56 Plymouth fins.

She is Ready

I like little ladies in red when old.
With piercing cardinal eyes
    they robin over snow for lingering elderberries,
    eagle over winter's gleaning ground,
    in flames fly out this mortal nest
    responding to a distant land,
    beloved sparrows known to God.

Little Ladies in Red

Cups clattering
    he tries,
    forgetting the cream,
    to make for the wife
    her coffee.
Tongue-tied
    her wishes punctuate
    their uncompleted sentences.
She no motor,
    he no mind,
They shuck possessions,
    pick the kernel roughly from the cob
    before the reaper comes,
Their only hope a stuttering laughter
    at their infantile complicity.

Cups Clattering

Seasons

In farthest north
  when people die in deep mid-winter
  after daring life
  despite the dumb dark wind,
The earth not ready to receive them,
  they lie spent in darkened sheds
  drying in suspended death.
In warming time of spring
  the earth receives their ceremonied husks.
In southern climes
  we die the same
  in slow and dire divorce.

Divorcèd Death

We are waiting, truly waiting
for warming sun,
dissolving rain,
to offer up the snow to sky,
to open up the road to town,
bring human faces to our door.
Hasty winter overturns our Advent,
traps our cozy expectations in the ice,
reveals the real time of human beings,
while down below the crowd goes shopping,
turning fervently the wheels of Christmas,
spinning future into past.
Not really looking for the baby in the wrappings,
voice drowned out in silent night,
and yet we find him,
yes, our Jesus, like a Russian doll,
the one with Nordic face,
no, underneath, the hillbilly Jew,
no, the farm boy from the Galilee,
the Yeshua,
the Yahweh-saves,
the one who never really was in Bethlehem,
the ancient wandering hope,
the tiny face a distant star whose earth we still can't see,
What we are waiting for in ice and snow.

Waiting

I fell in love with her this winter
    yet again.
Thirty years,
    where did they go,
    spinning in the vortex of our love,
    the beginning always present
    in the rush of dailyness?
In this hard winter
    even time is frozen,
    settling the froth
    to let me see into the waters
    of our birth
    and so begin again.

Love Again

Last night the basswood fell
    clean across the trail to the waterfall.
For twenty years we watched it leaning,
    roots hidden underneath the humus of ten thousand falls,
    locked within the splintered mantle of our mountain.
With every annual ring it yielded to the pull of earth
    until it rested in the arms of slender buckeyes and a cherry tree.
Holding it they danced five winters,
    let their leaves play in palpitation,
    change their dress from mossy green to calico
    before they fell in trusting premonition.
The night was still
    when its time came.
I with every creature heard it
    when the cherry and the buckeye
    received the basswood's death,
    and in embrace
    they fell together
    in our way.

The Fall

Earth gasping
    overheated from the race
    against our human grasping
    reeling from her broken pace
Melts ice to cool the fever
    slow the fire on the land
    turns winter into summer
    beaches dolphins on the strand
Inhales the noxious vapors
    breeding cancer in her lungs
    swallows refuse of her captors
    the bile rising to her tongue
Sends lilies up in mourning
    the rainbow as a pledge
    the cockroach as a warning
    the raven as a hedge.

Earth Gasping

This body from body
erupting
in water and blood
pleasure and hope
knows hunger and sucking, excretion and sleep.
This body of energy
leaping and jumping
dancing and running
lifting and swimming
knows motion and balance, upside and down.
This body of senses
with eyes seeing beauty and wonder
with ears hearing music and voices
with hands turning I into Us
knows love and delight beyond words.
These bodies now coupling
growing new bodies
their bodies one snake in one body immortal
know self beyond body, love beyond life.
These bodies now sitting and thinking
tenderly stroking the skins of their pasts
know time beyond space, sight beyond sense.
This body of memory
breath of a breath
at one with a body no longer its own
gives back to the earth
a life beyond bodies.

Body from Body

Dances

Earth dancing
    forty times
    around the sun,
    warming in reflection,
    turning with a tethered moon,
    a do-si-do in light and shadow,
Sun holding earth
    producing seasons succulent with mercy,
    tendered by the tango of their synchrony,
Stand
Still.
They wait,
    suspended in their gravity.
The universe quakes with applause,
    Clap! Clap!
    Bang! Bang!
Like master mistress of the Zen
    awake,
    they laugh,
    give thanks.
The emptiness of space
    is full of love.

Anniversary

In bibs and bill caps
burled men with sapling boys
strum and saw upon the stage,
fiddling with the old refrains,
plucking memories from our ears
like kernels from a dried out cob.
Pulsing with the promenade of age and innocence
we circle arms akimbo
under and out
tall and short
even and odd
young and old
swing our partners
now our corners
laughing as we listen to the call.
Corn meal under cloggers' soles
receives and fructifies communal aspirations,
raises hopes long buried in our hearts
that children would arise from scattered corn
and dance like fireflies before the rising moon.

Street Dance

If my love
    one only body had
But prestidigital
    kaleidoscoped
    in flesh appeared
    twice thrice transformed,
My only heart would find a way
    to wind twelve dozen fingers
    round her single soul
    to dance six thousand songs.

If My Love

Sparks
  break out the flue
  to breach the cosmic cinder glowing
  strike the stars
  where sky awake
  draws light upon
      the dark reposing earth,
  illuminates the hand of God
      warm cradling
      the hungry chasm of a universe
      convulsed in sleepy joy.
Here,
  my dear,
      let me give you the moon.

Sparks

The sky
    a bowl of jasperware
    he wore upon his head,
The clouds
    balloons of poetry
    that billowed from his smile,
The spring
    a wash of winter's crystals
    slathered on his lips,
And she
    her heart a mountain grove
    exploded into sparkling streams
    baptizing thirsty plains.

Lovespring

Rushing through the aisles
    eyes selecting spectacles,
    tongue tasting chocolate offerings,
    fingers pressing into leather gloves,
    arms arranging fine apparel on my shoulders,
    legs slipping into woolen slacks,
    slim feet exploring cordovans,
My hands
    in panting darkness
Pause
    around two silver shining coins
    to spend in her market.

Two Coins

Bridge the tender boundaries
    of the sexes,
    pitted in a see-saw
    warfare,
    one up
    one down.
Yin yang humans
    somewhat fitted
    seek in combat mockery
    contact
    real companionship
    veiled by the pretense
    of a crime.
He no she the apple tempted ate.

Southern Discomfort

Bonds broken
make a mending maze
where step
prosthetic
brother sister mother father grands and greats.
Half sightedly we
step,
son
and daughter
step,
mother
and father,
step
on stones across the raging river
step
on slippery banks to reach a quiet pool
step
upon the soles in other moccasins
step
in rhythm with the spiraling years
step
lively as the chairs are pulled away
to find
there was no ladder of affection to escape the maze,
only circles
where our bruised and bruising feet
find partners
in a mazing dance.

Steps

Like a Russian doll
    she wears each passage of her life in polymorphous coats.
She is the wise companion etched by years of circling suns,
    the woman burnished silver with accomplishment,
    the partner lighting household lamps,
the mate with auburn hair and radiant eyes,
    the mother of the squirming baby nestling at her breast,
    the college ingénue with witty tongue and voice of lark,
    the pigtail girl in the taffeta dress,
    the urchin hanging from her knees and laughing at her dad.
They dance,
    a manifold of nesting forms
    around the holy light within,
    each one the doll,
    each one the woman
    turning on the hidden center of her life.

Russian Doll

Beneath the crooked tired lamps
    flit frail taxis through neglected streets,
    worn out,
    cobbled into dereliction.
Lights dim,
    the conversations of the crowd begin to slur,
    sprightly motions atrophy in darkness,
    beaming smiles invert upon a palsied face.
Inside,
    the shop is closing down,
    the memories boxed.
Letters cram unopened files,
    undone acts released from hope.
Unanswered doorbells cease their clamor
    in the darkened corridors.
In rooms locked deep below
    a song survives within the night,
    the music still reverberates,
    the old films roll again.
Awake,
    a dancing power
    surges in the switches,
    convulsively explodes,
    leaps to universal audience,
    a shower of sparks
    in the fire of God.

A Dancing Power

Turnings

Already crossed,
the placid Shenandoahs
rippling over shallow hopes,
scouring out pit pocked illusions,
swirling into eddies calm with shade,
the wide Missouris,
brown with mountain sediments,
wrenching trees from cowering banks,
foaming over fertile plains,
the murky Jordans,
sluggish with our fear and loss,
purging us of putrifying pretension,
the rushing Rubicons,
ice-cold commitments cutting past from future glory,
all searching for the sea.
No bridge before us,
yet we crossed on stepping stones,
hopscotched miraculously
on sandbars fickle with flood,
navigated shifting shapes beneath the currents' spell,
pushed poles on fallen logs and wickered rafts,
swam among the flotsam of our fantasies,
borne up by foolish Christophers.
Have we not crossed enough?
Why do we faint before another river?
What nails our minds to memories on the walls behind?
Is it our tears within the flood before us?
Is it the trail on the other side?

Crossings

Doctor Einstein, I presume,
    discovered that the universe
    curves in upon itself.
But did he find that wisdom
    in the wilderness of space?
Or was he here enfolded
    in my lover's wakening arms?

Doctor Einstein

Glass melting shatters not,
    but slips beyond itself
    to forms unknown before the fire.
In color, shape, transparency
    it alchemizes in an instant,
    disembodies,
    amniotically creates
    a splendid crystal
    dazzling eye and hand and heart,
    a brilliance in new life
    from sand arising
    paying homage to the sun.

Glass Melting

He made pearls from his pain
    but never left his oyster.
In the darkness where the only light was hope,
    he laid down his opalescent sheen
    embraced in suffocating comfort,
    each tide
    each moon
    another shimmering coat
    of silent rumination
Until they smashed it,
    interrupting isolated beauty
    with kaleidoscopes of joy.

The Pearl

Tremblingly
    in stuttered whispers
    old now with regrets
    he rose before the table
    separating progeny.
His words were spoken
    one in thrall upon another,
"It is my death. We now divide the cup."
They split Leviathan asunder,
Creation in the grave.

Inheritance

The gift of ninety comes to us
    like snow soft crystals
            landing on a child's open hand,
    like song of meadowlark and thrush
            within a lightening dawn.
Not by strength
    or will
    or hope alone
    do we receive this time,
But as the bloom turns to the sunlight
    and the sea drinks in the rain
    do we receive this gift,
    all gift,
    as creatures living by the hand of God.

Gift of Ninety

Why do they leave us?
They told us they would leave if
    and they tried to leave
    if we had only
    but they wanted to if
    only they could go alone
    against our wishes that
    was why they had to
    go
And in an instant they were gone
    by rope or by bullet.

Why Do They Leave Us?

Fly pounded sparks explode
from metal
heavy
hard
smooth
blasted
sun seared
in the fire.
Smith fisted hammer falls,
Steam bellows from the buckets.
Crush handed bent
the tempered steel dances
on the anvil of God's mercy.

God's Mercy

I lay anxious fearing
    death's black hole,
    sucking into nothing all
                my work,
                        my thoughts,
                                my projects,
    grandiose and small.
My body lay in gurgles,
    its fragile circulation merely
    mindless worms
    below the muck.
My heart unmoored flopped back and forth
    between the terror of unending life
    and despair begot of finitude.
The mystery of a universe
    without a whence or whither
    paralyzed my consciousness.
My memory slipped in sadness,
    sought relief in nothingness,
    and failing,
    wept for loss of self.
And then my faithful lover,
    crossing over,
    touched me
    just so.

Meta-physical Comforts

The king towards his people is rightly compared to a father of children
and to a head of a body composed of divers members. — King James I

One day the expelled brothers joined forces, slew and ate the father,
and thus put an end to the father horde. — Sigmund Freud

Our king is kin
is kith
is kind
one of our kind
not kind
but kindred
of our king in dread
we kill
our king
our self.
Our regicide
a suicide
we side by side
rib over rib
sib over sib
kill sleeping head
and waking find
our mind in dread
of incest by a people blind.

Kin(g)

He lies who says he never lies
    where faithful men have never lain,
For he laid down his flowery words
    when she lay down in conjugation's loss.
Now, woman, lie in loss,
    lay up some dreams for compensation.
Think not he lied to you,
    for he has never lied to those with whom he's lain.
Or did he lie when she was laid?

Unconjugation

Wing of mercy
    touched,
    brushed,
    came over us,
    a blinding of our eyes.
Rain in rustled air
    washed away past wrongs,
    soaked up the stench of buried griefs,
    bathed the broken earth in miracle.
Rivers of blood,
    oceans of blood,
    passed over,
    claimed the rain,
    the wind,
    became again
    the waters of life.
People sought to bury it in news,
    but we knew close to heart
    that it was whispers
    of the Word.

A People Passing Over

That hole in the city's fabric
    seared with blasted crooked girders,
That hole in the ground
    created from the chaos of our aspirations,
That hole in the earth
    inebriate with septic lamentations
    lanced from bursting hearts of mercy.
That hole in our heart
    that lets our blood flood
    lifeless out upon the sand and stone,
This hole in humanity
    that frames the black infinity of death,
This hole unmended,
    mending,
    now reveals
    translucently
    the holiness of life.

After 9/11

O

the hole in the head

O

the wailing of the wounded women

O

the blood upon the Persian carpet

O

the ashes falling in the streets

O

the burning broken wounded flesh

O

the silence of the gentle voices

O

the dreaming lost to fear

O

the hole in the ground

O

the hole in our head.

O

She broke it open,
    split the shell,
    the crusted adamantine husk.
The mysteried megalith,
    hammered asunder,
    yawning forth imprisoned darkness,
    sparkled in the sun.
She laid it open,
    splendid geode of his love.

Nativity

They have taken my baby away.
    Three foreign men, they saddled him to stars.
    Men mad for ancient power claimed his birth in Bethlehem.
    My man, he rushed him off with me to distant sands.
    Old bearded men, they took him in the temple.
    Men blind with need besieged him in the village gates.
    Messiah men, they put a sword upon him.
First born, first taken,
    sacrificed to destinies beyond this place,
            this fertile earth,
            this home,
            this shop,
            these tools that could make of him a man —
They took us both away.

Mary's Cry

Turnings

There is a space between chapters,
    a crack in the spine.
Two pages meet
    and disappear
    into a hidden abyss
    where they are sewn invisibly together.

Between

You get on
confident,
saddle cinched,
bridle set just right, the teeth full forward,
reins in hand, fingers gripping left
then right.
The trail lies slant crooked cross the field where the old barn leans
with bulging hay and sentiments of harvest.
Today you're going to take the Love Lost Trail,
the one that wanders past the precipice
where the fated lovers fell in Indian tales.
She steps out walking,
then a trot and canter,
but suddenly she takes the gate into the Devil's Britches Trail
up the stony steps and down the creek beside the ancient hemlocks
to the switchback where the Devil lost his pants and let the lovers go.
Adjusted to the steeper climb, the aromatic pungency,
the moisture oozing from the rocks,
the slower pace,
the torpid rhythm of her shoes,
you settle back to see the view until
you come upon a gushing rivulet,
dismount,
and cup a shimmering icy drink from falling waters,
a place where you had never been.
Then back on,
your knees and hands in firm command
you find the gap out to the bald.
Skimming over grasses at a smoother breezy pace
you wind back down the mountain past the cut-off to Persimmon Grove,
emerge flush breathless right beside the leaning barn.

Writer's Way

To turn, turn will be our delight,
'till by turning, turning, we come 'round right.

Traditional Shaker song,
"Simple Gifts," by Joseph Brackett Jr.

About the Author

William Everett's thirty years of teaching, research, and writing in Christian ethics took him to Catholic and Protestant seminaries in Milwaukee, Atlanta, and Boston as well as Germany, India, and South Africa. His writings explored issues of marriage and family, religion and law, ecology, and the ethical dimensions of worship and symbolism. In 2001 he turned full time to his passion for poetic writing and woodworking.

In his first work of fiction, *Red Clay, Blood River* (2008), he put his inter-continental experience in the service of an historical novel about connections between America's "Trail of Tears" and South Africa's "Great Trek." Written from an ecological standpoint, in which Earth is the narrator, it explores themes of estrangement, oppression, memory, and reconciliation.

This first volume of his poems leads us from narrative to the startling array of images at the heart of his writing. His poetry often reflects the cadences, symbolism, and language of liturgies and the Bible, just as his round communion tables and other furniture inspire a number of chapels and churches.

He and his wife Sylvia, a visual artist, reside in the Great Smoky Mountains of western North Carolina. Their artistic work can be seen at www.WisdomsTable.net. He journals regularly at www.WilliamEverett.com.